# FROGS, FRAGS & KISSES

*tanka, haiku, limericks and*
*other short poems*

## Eric G. Müller

*Apprentice House*
*Loyola University Maryland*
*Baltimore, Maryland*

First Edition

Printed in the United States of America

Paperback ISBN: 978-1-62720-061-5
E-book ISBN: 978-1-62720-062-2

Design by Kelley Murphy


Published by Apprentice House

Apprentice House
Loyola University Maryland
4501 N. Charles Street
Baltimore, MD 21210
410.617.5265 • 410.617.2198 (fax)
www.ApprenticeHouse.com
info@ApprenticeHouse.com

"This marvelous collection of tanka, frags, haiku, and limericks reminds me of the gem-like quality of all small things in the world. Whether it's a deeply profound meditation on life and death, or a light, deft vignette showing us fat crows in bare trees or a boat in the harbor, or simply a conversation with a hibiscus, each of Eric Müller's poems sparkles and glows with color, feeling, and story."

> — Eliot Winslow, award winning author of *Poems from the Oasis, What Would You Do If There Was Nothing You Had To Do?* and other books

*   *   *

"*Frogs, Frags and Kisses* is a recipe for fun winter reading: a dash of Edward Lear,a sprinkle of Ogden Nash, and some soulful stirring."

> — April Zipser, author and editor at Prolific Press

*   *   *

"A rich collection of "short form poems": wise, mischievous, and healing. An enticing invitation to enter into play with the small and the big, and at once to ponder well.""

> — Douglas Sloan, Professor of History and Education Emeritus, Teachers College, Columbia University

*   *   *

"The tankas, haiku, limericks, and "frags" in Eric Müller's collection offer moments of whimsy, of wisdom, and of observation that's been stripped clean of pretense. It is clear that their creator is enamored of and humbled by being alive. His humility is reassuring, his amore invigorating. Each small poem is a shot in the arm."

> —Julianna Spallholz, author of *The State of Kansas*

dedicated to the small in all things big
and the big in all things small

and my family

# contents

preface....1

tanka..............5

frags...................29

haiku......................61

limericks........................69

acknowledgments................87

publication credits.....................88

about the author..............................89

# preface

It took me years to get into the habit of carrying a little notebook with me wherever I went, as suggested by so many writers. My only regret is that I did not start sooner. It serves as a little thought basket into which I can place the chance observations, insights, ideas, sudden inspirations, scraps of conversations or anything else I might spy, find, receive, uncover or pluck from the side of the road as I zigzag my way through life. Back home, I can sift through the findings, categorize, organize and polish them. Eventually, they make their way into my novels, short stories, articles or poems.

But numerous thought fragments and minimalistic poems often remain unused and forgotten in these little notebooks piling up on the left-hand corner of my windowsill, next to my concertina-playing garden gnome. Over the last two years, I started going through the miscellaneous notebooks with an eye on all the poetic 'frags' I might find. I was surprised how many completed short form poems I came across.

Poetic fragments and haiku have always found their

way into my notebooks. The habit of writing limericks and tanka is more recent. They are polarities of sorts. In the tanka, I explore the more numinous aspects of the world and my inner life, whereas the limericks offer the needed balance of levity and humor. Both forms allow me to 'play' with the language, the images and its innate musicality. I chose to stick to the strict forms of the tanka, haiku and limericks. The structure was a welcome mold that allowed the 'play impulse' (Friedrich Schiller), more room. It was like stepping into a sandbox of words, in which I could build my little worlds. I've also called these brief poems my 'in-between poems,' because they have served as relaxants, fillers or therapeutic thought pills that while away the little moments amid the greater tasks of life, such as my vocation as an educator or the writing of my novels or long poems.

I'd pen them at the mall, airport, bus terminal, or dentist while waiting for life to move on. They are dedicated to the little moments that could easily be lost to distraction or plain boredom. But every moment counts, and there's something more to be found in the most mundane instances: fleeting epiphanies or ephemeral revelations that pass us by if we let them or don't pay heed.

Some of these micro-poems were kneaded in the dead of night - those harsh insomniac eternities that can easily send life's realities into harmful disproportions, where useless, repetitive thoughts upset one's mental equilibrium, where we can easily sink into our nether regions: our ugly self that likes to find fault and criticize. These short-shorts, which I commit to memory until the following morning, have often served as a sure antidote to my insomnia, turning a potentially negative frame of mind into a positive.

Taking these tanka, fragments, haiku and limericks from the obscurity of the notebooks (and other odd scraps of paper) and compiling them into a book has confirmed for me once again the importance of the small things in the world - the seemingly inconsequential times of our lives. Everything counts. It all has its place: the big as much as the small.

*- Eric G. Müller*

# tanka

Dawn's waking moment
lets fingers fondle locks
while dreams cling to hair –
weight of day's work lies ahead
she sighs and furrows her face

Dusk looks down, knowing
too much work is left undone
which he's learned to bear –
fatigue shows in his many trials
chiseled deep into his beard

Night in naked sleep
births an owl between her legs
ignores the fright mask
that lies empty to her left
while wisdom stares wide awake

Day twists like a snake
from the pain of his failures
and those still to come –
puzzled eyes pierce the distance
where he'll meet his future self

he waits as she cleans
dreading when she'll stop to talk
about what happened –
a finch bumps against the window
and falls dead out on the deck


two moons face five stars
by the elbow-arched bridge
that led me to you
through the park with ponds and pines
tears refract my memory

an owl and angel
fold wings and knowingly nod
through the still of night
before and after each day
through which people rush and fume


I push through the crowd
to find a place to listen
but none says *stop now*
so I give way to the walk
hearing music in the noise

the girl skips out to play
with the neighbors and their dolls
happy in her heart –
but she's met by a father
who plays, breaks and discards her

insomnia strikes
in many shades of gloom
from soft, blunt to sharp –
in the wait I bend the black –
a cave from which I labor

a lump of white sugar
held between thumb and forefinger
above steaming tea –
I fall, dissolve and vanish
to sweeten and warm your life


fine flakes of moonlight
cast the night into a fest
of shades uncovered
the unknown stripped of fear
shows gardens instead of graves

bottles in a shed
none the same as the other
in shape and color
sun gives glimpse of old glory
filled with feasts' liquid laughter

moving here and there
uprooted and made homeless
always a stranger
must make everyplace my own
find home in the world within

on the floor he sits
in the dirt by the ashes
the fire is dead
pine wood burns quicker than oak
no kindling left in bin

fleeing the bad feel
he makes small talk and tells jokes
but she does not laugh
a skunk from the woods
leaves his mark and slinks away

he turns to the blackboard
his forehead knocks the slate
fingers crush the chalk
all the children have gone home
they do not see their teacher weep



she looks to the floor
right through the mandala tiles
to a hidden wish
her sneakers want to move on
and they squeak as she obeys

my head is a burl
knotty lump of tangled thoughts
waiting for a lathe
I enter a gallery
the paintings are panes in oils

in need of some *Ting*
Chinese for stop, rest or pause
I climb a spinney
cool shade wraps my fractured day
and swaying green is my salve

active all day long
still I think it's not enough
and do one more thing –
hummingbird by the fuchsia
a lamb bleats in the valley


I enter people
and hear them from the inside
all their joys and pain
major and minor music
to which my ears are open

there is something else
always at the ready
waiting to flow in
to give us what we need
but we're not always ready

full jug of water
on a rock in a big field
thirsty crowd stands still
water's poured into the earth
all sigh, go home, and rain comes

in life's hourglass
a silent stream of sand falls
on my naked skin
soft kisses of raspberries
or short, sharp shots of arrows

pain we don't forget
though we're often in denial
still, it shows itself –
the spirit we do forget
there's no denying that

faces in a crowd
tend to look like animals
they're easy to spot
mammals, reptiles, insects, fish
we don't like to face ourselves


puss of vanity
is a blemish to us all
if left unheeded
it will fester in our sleep
and release a big, bad stink

thoughts shoot from my head
pecked off by crows in mid flight
flocks more come to feed
flapping dark clouds screeching fear
must change to feed nightingales


if we listen for
what the moment demands
we'll know what to do –
she trips and falls to the ground
I bend down and help her up

to fulfill our tasks
with human humility
is to feel fulfilled
she smiled as she stepped on stage
not knowing who put her there


a tiny bottle
in the shape of a cello
on the window sill
the sun shines through its green glass
and sorrow gives way to sound

mostly I just dream
it's less a curse than a gift
pages to open
swirling swarms of butterflies
my stories painted on wings

guitar and soft voice
cars and clouds pass by outside
coffee tightens dreams
tree tattoo on singer's back
sways as she strums joy and calm

a quick reminder –
be compassionate, loving
warm and interested
and we'll change the whole wide world
it really is that simple


he fears dusk and sleep
tossing on grit and granite
blood whipped by ice winds
at work he smiles and cracks jokes
no one sees his dark-ringed eyes

always fresh taboos
no matter the number smashed
baby 'boos jump up
strutting catwalks with halos
swanky clothes for fat empress




Mary, true to the name
cries bitter tears for her Son
to fill Sorrow's seas
on which the Fisherking sails
La Mer, the grief of Mary

my baby, my man
my suffering son, my lamb
you're light on my lap
a heavy world in my heart
your life to come keeps me calm

for those who can not
I will have to learn to speak
so through me they can
I in turn look to others
who'll lead me where I can not

plagued by outer things
the noise, the pain – discomforts
plagued by inner things
horror flick self projected
relationships unsolved


at birth we're severed
separation is our sin
we're torn asunder
always aching to unite
through love that gives us pleasure

blueing of the day
wakes my senses to the world
return from raised sky
birds chirp as I sip my tea
dreams fade as stars slip from view


fine dust on fingers
looking through box of photos
so much forgotten
through the layers to his youth
once done he washes his hands

we're at the mercy
of others every second
their help, trust or hate
you and I are the others –
must raise trust, care and mercy


through café window
solid snow slows passing traffic
fat crows in bare trees
red poinsettia on table
new life warms under white stars

when he ground his teeth
he heard music in his ears
clear as through a fog
like when a diamond needle
is placed on a vinyl groove


dried streaks down her cheeks
on a boat in the harbor
waiting on the deck
last call before departure
more tears for lost love, new life

# frags

at every moment we're
      different,
but how
      different
are we at every moment?

we think we're covered
but we're naked still

broken bicycle
tired eyes
lion in the wind
humming waitress
guilt in the gutter
cobbled history
Lolita frown
sliced space
60 Seconds –
time's up

places of pain and death
are only worth visiting
if those who suffered
are redeemed by our visit


the anonymity
of a public place
is as comforting
as the intimacy
of time at home


baby Bacchus
squats on a swan
gobbling grapes
and smiling slightly
like the Buddha

the undertone
of the all-day-long
is my inadequacy
that transposes
as guilt


the little arched chirrup
of the tufted titmouse
greeted me
as I drank my tea
leaving me a tad more free


Man
Who-man
Woo-man
War-man
Woe-man
Womb-man
Woman

my past
is the compost
that nourishes
the bed in which
I'm presently planted –
waiting for me
to wake and walk
the earth, which is
my future




if self-absorption
        leads to
self-development
        then it
might be worth it




it's not worth mentioning, except
emotions get spilled, words go astray
and something is broken

"Love too needs practice,"
 said the teacher
 as she tolerantly
 gauged the tipping point
 of her own level of love




who cares?
nobody cares!
but keep on caring
till somebody cares




umbrella is an opening thing
that wants closure and a good
shake at the end of it all

"Why do you have the 6 of hearts
  tacked to your wall?"
"Because seven is the number of perfection
  and the heart is the symbol of love.
  The six reminds me that I'm always falling short."
"Sounds weirdly esoteric."
"Want to know about my broken balalaika
  dangling from the ceiling?"


I am
  I aim
    High name
      Sky fame
Skill, strength and target in-sight
      My shame
    Must tame
  Hot flame
I am

she slashed into my sleep
with her box-cutter bark

"Just be yourself,"
 said the self made man

how long will it take
before we realize
    how important it is
    how we do
what we do
in the world?

to empty into emptiness
is to expand into nothing
in the hope of finding something

when things don't
matter anymore
it's a kind of death
that liberates

the river bed will soon dry out
but it's running still
and that's all that matters now

hi hibiscus
sweet biscuit
for the eye


I have nothing much to say
but I say it anyway – in case
something more slips in


we're all
somnolent figures
in a wounded
landscape
and those most
lost are those
who think
they aren't

the true I
is invisible
but more real
than the hardest matter



sense the future
and mix that
with common sense



to ease the
pain of waiting
practice
resting
which permeates
the waiting
with ease

yes!
I do want –
but more than that
I want
not to want




yes is more
and
no is a door
that
            opens
when you accept
the door that's
            shut




there should be
a little bit of
Grail
in everything
we do

yes
it's true
I am a monk
of the mundane
sensing my surroundings
afresh at every moment
reveling in the riches
while admitting
my poverty


a pile of wood
neatly stacked against
the side of the house
under the porch –
bleeding


she stunk her way to the top
her success turned out a flop

the feet step
up the stairs
while
the head gets
lost in threads
and
the lungs turn
to boulders
which
starve the heart
of new blood
telling
me to turn
around and start
again


how we think of others
and ourselves
determines
all social behavior that
severs
or unites us

one by one
I let things
go

until at last
I find
myself

and when I do
I won't let
go


there's fake
and reality –
we live our lives
between the two


youth hanging out in the hallway
snails on a wet log

if you want
to change the
visible
become
invisible

if you
work with the
invisible
you can change the
visible



what's the
color of
blood
when freed
of the last drop of
selfishness?

there's so much
to drag us
down –
times we've
failed –
times others have
failed us

there's so much
more
to lift us up –
times we've
succeeded –
times others have
helped us
succeed

there is no
equality on this earth
because we have to
gain equality in the spirit
which will ensure
equality on this earth

if the swan
sings more beautifully
when death
approaches
then let me
live each moment
as if death
is near –
and, in truth
it always is


it means
less and less
to me
what once meant
more and more –
and what once
seemed less
now means more

always on the
lookout
for natural
stimulants
that move to
inquire

always on the
look-in
for mystic
stimulants
that
inspire

and always
vice versa


I've taken gently to
stretching my hands
toward things of
beauty
in a gesture of thankful
blessing

. . . . . . . . . . . . . . . . . . . . . . . . . . . . . . . . . . . . . . . . . . . . . . . . . . . . . . . . . . . . . . . . . . . . . . . . . . . . . . . . . . . . . . . . . . . .

"Who is God?"
said the poet who'd
lost the Word

"Where is God?"
said the poet
in search of the Word

"I found the Word!"
said the poet
beginning to create




it's not a
matter of learning, but
    changing
through learning

"Christians
are hated
because most
Christians
are not very
Christian,"
said the
Christian


the man with the accordion
in front of the basilica
gets soaked with the
six-o' clock downpour
of rain and tolling bells... still
he plays on unperturbed
as he does through all
the other sonic disturbances to
his music that is our own,
if we could only listen
        carefully
enough

we love the known
but there was a time
when it was unknown –
treat the unknown
as a future treat!


I'm looking
for that place
where I can face
forward and feel
my past
make sense
in relation to the
whole


let anything ugly
in the world
be the impetus
to create something
beautiful

there are only a few heroes
left in my life –
the ones I had
have disappointed me
but more than ever
I see a hero
in everyone
I meet


how easy it is
to offend –
how useless
to defend –
how difficult
to mend
the hurt
which has harmed
our ease

just being
yourself
is a
confession
   *or in other words*
an honest word
spoken
is an ad-mission
of sorts


note how many
   things go right
or           wrong
   each day
and yet you might
be surprised
to learn how many
   things go right
even on  the  worst  of  days

each journey, a pilgrimage
to Walmart or to Mecca
to Hudson or the Holy Land
to work or to war
to the fridge or the Fijis
to the basement or the Bahamas –
once we think this way
that we're pilgrims on a journey
then – wherever we go –
we'll never move the same again


more than you think
the earth is changed
by the way we look

how the future will look
will depend on how we look
now – in the present

which is the result
of past looking
i.e. compounded sensing

someone's singing
round the corner
just for the fun of it

how rare it is
for someone to sing
just for the fun of it


there's always
something demanded
            of us
and when there isn't
it's only because
room is made
for something
that's demanded
            of us

epiphanies have gone
out of fashion –
people will start
having them again
when fashions
no longer count


"Simplify and deepen,"
said the nurse nonchalantly
and I found it easy
to simplify
but not to deepen


if you want to
        hear more music
                listen to less music

and when it's time
the champion will come
to move your work
(when it's ripe and ready)
into the world
where it will do its work
that you'd wished it would


spear it
and follow the arc
from your center
toward the mark
that aches for
spirit


freedom, it walks, it walks...
walks on the long
the long, long road
of necessity

if my poems
were pills
I'd want them
to perk you up –
give you a kick
in the right direction
do whatever's necessary
to lure you back
into life –
if my poems
were pills,
I'd want them to
taste good too

"You'd change yourself too
if you only knew
what others think of you,"
said the clown with a frown

when things begin
there is no sin
but sometimes
things begin with sin


in perspective
        drawing
it's all about the
        angle

it's all about the
        angle
if we want to gain
        perspective


the world is my
        installation
                I translate with
                        words

I'm a double reject
cast down the john
though I'm spurned on
to eject another try
to shoot for more effect –
and damn the cry
of a triple flush

they meet at the apple tree
peacock spreads his feathery fan

she breathed in the stars
and remembered the footprints
that pressed into the red earth road
pushing her on to limb the ground
having breathed in the stars

I'm tired
of lying awake

and when finally
I fall asleep

it's time
to wake up


yellow clouds
of pollen
on the parquet floor
from the bouquet of sunflowers
around which we sit
trying to solve our problems

## THREE BOLD WORDS

**! !!!! !!!**

stared at him    and he
                fell
                to
                his
                knee
       and shouted

**!YesSheDoes! !SheDoes!**

# haiku

cool breath of AC
the itch of mosquito bites
time to go home now

the scream of a child
in the hallways of a dream
comes to mind as me

my world and your world
maybe they will intersect
in a way they have

exit signs in red
mock me as I sit and wait
for it all to end


man with umbrella
sneezes like a tuba burst
rain stops and sun shines


yes, we can harden
must steel myself from the pain
it makes loving hard

insignificant?
life blood pulses through my veins
that's significant


anger in the streets
igniting conflagration
heat of the moment


daily miracles
cookie rests on rubber band
tasty and a stretch

do good to others
on days you don't like yourself
and you'll feel better


one by one they stand
and add their voice to the song
that silences guns


cappuccino kiss
a promise of more to come
pleasure's secret missive

as long as you try
don't count your battles as lost
though you feel you've failed


we know it takes time
all the things we want to do
the moment threatened


black-capped chickadee
lands on a dead sunflower
erect and swaying

he's an open book
people pass by not reading
day's wind turn pages


a flute, a violin
they play perfectly in tune
no hint of divorce


we're separated
from the moment we're born
daily choice to bond

in failure we fall
waking up to our own pain
rise of consciousness


he folds his glasses
puts them down and turns off lamp
sinks into dark hole


in the tight meantime
warm air rises over cold
as love always does

sensitivity
to understand each other
anachronism

my bad memory
made good by interest in all
loving the moment

hot water bottle
my teddy bear on cold nights
dead haddock at dawn

# limericks

there was a blonde in pink
who dreamed of wearing mink
she looked around
and quickly found
a man she could hook with a wink

Hemingway had a cat with six toes
who purred and softened his woes
she sat on his lap
and didn't give a crap
when he slipped off to Sloppy Joe's

every morning at four
I can't sleep no more
I burn, I churn
twist and turn
wracked by thoughts to the core

there was a tough guy with a truck
who powered his horses through muck
grinding the gears
he had no fears
till he tried to reverse and got stuck

clutch those low clouds from the sky
and fashion yourself a bowtie
you'll stand more erect
sure to detect
how people will say, *Oh my!*

behind the shed in the dark
he heard the song of a lark
how could that be
nothing's for free
so he gave up his pride for his heart

she loved to ride in her limousine
which made her feel like a queen
but then she died
the chauffeur cried
and sped off with a long-legged teen


there was a man from Penublay
who would always say, *I say*
*I say,* he said,
*I say*, he said,
*Don't you run away, I say.*

there was an old wench in his room
who made him sigh and swoon
while on his knees
spotting her fleas
she seduced him with her perfume

on the day he received his promotion
his wife caused a great big commotion
*You're never at home*
*you leave me alone*
*and you owe it to all my devotion*

his loud and coruscating wit
put her into a frightful fit
she showed him the door
shouting – *Can't stand it no more* –
which didn't perturb him one bit


born with a smile on his face
he agreed, for once, to give chase
he didn't get far
got hit by a car
and died for a girl called Grace

a mole lived alone in a hole
all broken in body and soul
in order to mend
he wanted a friend
but wouldn't leave his hole for that goal




she came and said, *I'm Penny*.
I ordered and said, *I'm Lenny.*
she brought the drink
and gave me a wink
and that night we had fun making Jenny

something bad is about to take place
we'll only be saved by Grace
let's sing a song
and help her along
to make this a happy space

it's time to stop the fight
no matter who's in the right
before too long
we'll both be wrong
and nothing will make it right

I wait for the day to start
and slip into my part
put on a face
join the race
till I reenter my heart in the dark


Missy met Jones in New York
his eyes were those of a hawk
he plunged his talons
into her soft melons
and plugged her tight with his cork

there was a diner no finer
with a waitress who couldn't be kinder
she gave it her all
at your beck and call
and still I'm trying to find her

slowly he slouched into school
wearing shades and looking real cool
he had no care
and nothing was fair
but in his heart he felt like a fool

under the Eiffel Tower
she stood waiting for over an hour
he was a no-show
she started to go
when he ran up and gave her a flower

he's got tired and watery eyes
and still he throws around knives
he doesn't take aim
but all the same
he hits the mark and thrives

he boxed my ears and laughed
I thought he was quite daft
he slapped some more
I fell on the floor
and couldn't get up till I barfed

he was a very bad man
who loved the glitz and glam
he forgot his true goal
and lost his soul
and didn't give a damn

in the bathroom next to the towels
there's a poodle who always growls
what to do
when you go to the loo
and get bit while you're moving your bowels


naturally the man is wrong
to keep silent for so long
it drives me insane
but it's all in vain
for now he's gone off to Hong Kong

he carried curry to Carrie
and said his name was Gary
*a delicious spice*
*goes well with rice*
*you and I should marry*

a girl from Tennessee
buzzed by like a bumblebee
she knew what to do
for me and you
by making us feel more free

listen to me you fool
I hear you're way too cruel
you gotta be kind
and then you'll find
they'll think you are quite cool

the monkey swung through the trees
to help rid his friend of fleas
he picked them out
but was in doubt
when itching robbed his ease

she sat on a wall and thought
about all the things she'd been taught
she let out a sigh
and wondered why
she still felt so stupid and caught

the parrot on top of the cage
held forth like a wise old sage
he spoke without fear
and fluidly clear
even when spouting his rage

I don't care what you say
we'll do what's right today
I'll prove to you
we'll carry it through
we'll get rid of the things in the way

a baboon sat on a dune
in the jolly month of June
sipping gin
with a silly grin
while barking his way to the moon

# acknowledgments

Putting a book into the world takes the concerted effort of many people. I am full of gratitude to every person who helped with this project. Appreciation and thanks go to the entire editorial team at Apprentice House, especially Rachel Dooley, Kayla McKnight, designer Kelley Murphy, and publisher Kevin Atticks. Their enthusiasm and warmth for my compilation shone through at every step. It was a great pleasure working with them. Moreover, I would like to thank the editors of the magazines, anthologies and journals where some of these poems first appeared. I'd also like to extend my thanks to Matthew Müller for his careful reading of the poems and his pertinent comments. And, as always, I wish to express my gratefulness to my wife, Martina Müller, for her ongoing support and helpful insights. She was often close by while I wrote these short poems, and knows the finer layers in which they are wrapped.

# **publication credits**

Some of the poems first appeared in the following publications: *Inner Art Journal; A Hundred Gourds; The Mindful Word; Dressing Room Poetry; Chrysanthemum; Boston Literary Magazine; The Momo Reader; Local Gems Poetry Press; Fortunates; Poetry Pacific; Short, Fast and Deadly; Clutching at Straws; Eunoia Review; Blink Ink; 3 lines poems; Yes, Poetry; 50 Haikus; a handful of stones; A Blackbird Sings, a book of short poems; The Mind[less] Muse.*

# about the author

**Eric G. Müller** studied literature and history at the University of the Witwatersrand, Johannesburg, South Africa. He continued his studies in England and Germany, where he specialized in drama and music education. Together with his family, he moved to Eugene, Oregon, where he taught for eight years. Currently, he is living in upstate New York, teaching music, drama, English literature and creative writing. He has written two novels, *Rites of Rock* (Adonis Press, 2005) and *Meet Me at the Met* (Plain View Press, 2010), as well as a collection of poetry, *Coffee on the Piano for You* (Adonis Press, 2008). His most recent publications include *The Invisible Boat* (Waldorf Publications, 2013), a book for children, and *Drops on the Water: Stories about Growing Up from a Father and Son* (AH, Loyola University, Baltimore, 2014). Poetry, articles and short stories have appeared in many journals, anthologies and magazines. www.ericgmuller.com

Apprentice House is the country's only campus-based, student-staffed book publishing company. Directed by professors and industry professionals, it is a nonprofit activity of the Communication Department at Loyola University Maryland.

Using state-of-the-art technology and an experiential learning model of education, Apprentice House publishes books in untraditional ways. This dual responsibility as publishers and educators creates an unprecedented collaborative environment among faculty and students, while teaching tomorrow's editors, designers, and marketers.

Outside of class, progress on book projects is carried forth by the AH Book Publishing Club, a co-curricular campus organization supported by Loyola University Maryland's Office of Student Activities.

Eclectic and provocative, Apprentice House titles intend to entertain as well as spark dialogue on a variety of topics. Financial contributions to sustain the press's work are welcomed. Contributions are tax deductible to the fullest extent allowed by the IRS.

To learn more about Apprentice House books or to obtain submission guidelines, please visit www.apprenticehouse.com.

Apprentice House
Communication Department
Loyola University Maryland
4501 N. Charles Street
Baltimore, MD 21210
Ph: 410-617-5265 • Fax: 410-617-2198
info@apprenticehouse.com • www.apprenticehouse.com

www.ingramcontent.com/pod-product-compliance
Lightning Source LLC
Chambersburg PA
CBHW072044040426
42447CB00012BB/3005